YPS

YESHIVA PIRCHEI SHOSHANIM
ישיבת פרחי שושנים

Pirchei Publishing
146 Village Path / P.O. Box 708
Lakewood, New Jersey 08701
(732) 370-3344
www.shulchanaruch.com

Edited & Compiled by YPS:
Rabbi Shaul Danyiel & Rabbi Ari Montanari
www.lionsden.info/YPS

Science of Kabbalah – Lesson One
Introduction

YPS
YESHIVA PIRCHEI SHOSHANIM

Written by: Rabbi Yitzchak Michaelson

164 Village Path, Lakewood NJ 08701 732.370.3344
164 Rabbi Akiva, Bnei Brak, 03.616.6340

Outline of This Lesson:

1. Introduction

2. Early Study of the Universe

3. Post Newtonian Cosmology

4. Scientific Account of Creation

5. Does the Gap Narrow?

6. Review Questions

7. Review Answers

Introduction

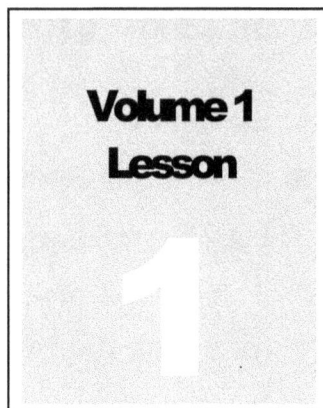

Volume 1
Lesson

1

When most people hear the word *Kabbalah*[1] today, they either dismiss it as some type of fad, or connect it with its red string bracelets, Kabbalah holy water, and star converts, like Madonna. Other's think of it simply as a mystical form of Judaism that carries with it a stringent adherence to the minutiae of laws. However, nothing could be further from the truth.

Kabbalah is neither a fad, nor is it a religion. The very word Kabbalah is the Hebrew word for "receiving." Instead, Kabbalah is a science and based on its definition of "receiving," should be interpreted as the *Science of Reception*! Regardless of what one hears, this science was never meant to be available to only a select few with the proper credentials. As you will learn throughout these lessons, there is a science and wisdom that is meant to bring transformation to those who study it, and is now open and available to all humankind, especially tp the individual searching for spirituality.

There is an emptiness that every individual has experienced at one time or another, and this then drives toward a path of spirituality. It originates from their soul's desire for connection and correction.

---

[1] *The Hebrew word for "receiving."*

Haven't we all at one time or another asked ourselves these questions?

Who am I? Why am I here? What is my purpose in life?

The science of Kabbalah reveals the answers to these questions, and so many more. The goal of anyone seeking to study this ancient wisdom is to answer those questions, determine the origin of life, creation, including a search for self. Ultimately, there is a desire stirred up within the individual to use the answers to these ancient questions in order to understand the proper path to take to achieve one's goals in life.

Year after year people look for that next something to fill the void that exists within them, and yet whatever that next something is, it never seems to bring the satisfaction intended. Then, when our desires are left unfulfilled, we are unsatisfied, disillusioned, and begin filling our empty space with other distractions. Some look to drugs, alcohol, sex, and other activities in order to allow them to escape from their problems and the troubles that exist in the world around them. They are simply looking for the answer to the meaning of life, rather than being satisfied with carving out an unfulfilling existence, that allows them to simply skate through life.

The next fancy car, big house, or latest technology toy may make life easier to bear, but most people soon tire of these material things, because they are looking for something else. They are seeking to discover something higher.

Many will try the latest self-help books. Another might turn to some TV guru, or the latest snake oil salesman pitching some philosophical or psychological answer to all of their problems.

However, none of these will supply the answers, because they do not get to the root of the problem, which is providing a purpose for life. This question can only be answered when an individual chooses to search from within, rather than searching for external solutions.

When you realize that you have exhausted yourself in this life and that nothing in this material world interests you anymore, then you are ready to truly "receive."

If you are such a person, then prepare to join us on a journey toward enlightenment. The reception of an ancient wisdom that will change your life from the inside out. This is the "Science of Kabbalah."

Note: The famous teachers of Kabbalah used different names to represent God. The Ari, Rabbi Yitzchak Luria stated, *"No thought can grasp Him. The One is essentially unknowable."*

Keeping in mind that some people have issues with the term God, if you have negative emotions towards its use, feel free to use whatever you are comfortable with. For instance, *"The Light, A Higher Power, The Power of Love, The Source of Creation, The One, etc."*

The Early Study of the Universe

To understand Kabbalah as a science, we must first look at how earlier scientists influenced and were influenced by this most ancient of wisdoms.

Let's explore for a minute the life of "Sir Isaac Newton," considered to be one of the greatest scientists that ever lived. In addition to being a scientist, he was a theologian. He revolutionized physics, mathematics, and astronomy in the 17th and 18th century. He laid the foundation for most of classical mechanics—with the principal of universal gravitation and the three laws of motion bearing his name. The image below was found in documents that appeared as part of his library. It bears his elementary attempt at writing a sentence in Hebrew on the second line of the document.

These words are at the end of a prayer called *Keri'at Shema*[2] (Reading of Shema) in the daily prayers of Judaism. The words that appear are the ones shown in the image below

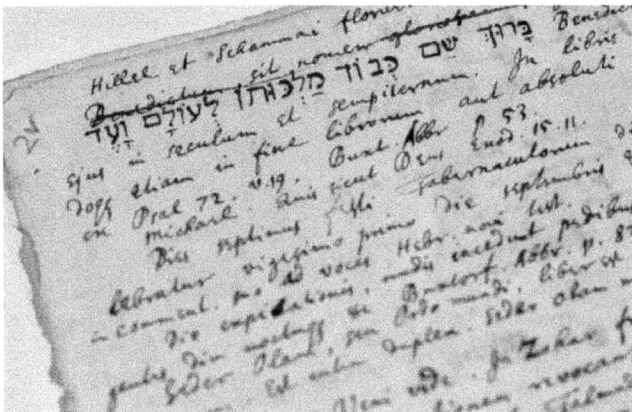

2

The transliteration of the above words are, "*Baruch Shem Kevod Malchuto Le'Olam Va'ed*"

The simple meaning of these words are typically translated as:

"*Blessed is the name of His glorious kingdom forever and ever.*"

Most people would never know that someone like Sir Isaac Newton, who had such an impact on science, viewed much of what he studied through the lens of Kabbalah. Newton's theological manuscripts that are now housed in Jerusalem were once shown to Albert Einstein. Despite the fact that it was September 1940 and he was already involved himself with an apocalyptic enterprise, he took the trouble to compose a letter praising the papers for the insight they afforded into Newton's geistige Werkstatt, his "spiritual workshop."

The image on the right is a page from a Latin translation of the Zohar[3], ascribed to Isaac Newton.

In the book, "The Religion of Isaac Newton," Frank E. Manuel wrote that "*Isaac Newton was convinced that Moses possessed the knowledge of all scientific secrets.*" Dr Seth Pancoast wrote that "*Isaac Newton was led to the discovery of physical laws (forces of gravitation and repulsion) through the study of Kabbalah.*"

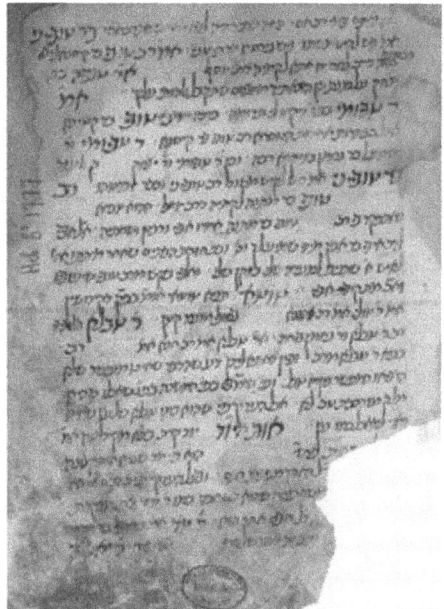

---

[3] The **Zohar** (Hebrew: זהר, lit. "Splendor" or "Radiance") is the foundational work in the literature of Jewish wisdom known as Kabbalah

A Latin translation of The Book of Zohar (Kabbalah Denudata), was found in Newton's library and is currently kept at the Trinity College in Cambridge. Isaac Newton based his scientific research on philosophical principles.

In particular, Newton wrote: *"In my books I laid down the principles of philosophy that are not purely philosophical, but also mathematical, which can serve as the basis for discussing physical matters. So that they don't seem fruitless, I accompanied them with some physical explanations.[4]"*

A contemporary of Newton, Francis Bacon wrote this, to show the separation that existed between science and theology of the day: *"Let no man upon a weak conceit of sobriety or an ill-applied moderation think or maintain, that a man can search too far, or be too well studied in the book of God's word, or in the book of God's works, divinity or philosophy; but rather let men endeavor an endless progress or proficiency in both; only let men beware that they apply both to charity, and not to swelling; to use, and not to ostentation; and again, that they do not unwisely mingle or confound these learning's together.[5]"*

Other great scientists of the time in trying to maintain the separation between the two worlds of religion and science also studied this type of wisdom.

Frank E. Manuel continues in his book *"The Religion of Isaac Newton,"* that Galileo and Kepler had based their fundamental arguments on an ancient dictum of scriptural interpretation by the Jewish sages, *"The Bible speaks in the language of everyman."*

---

[4] (Newton I., Mathematical Principles of Natural Philosophy, 1686, V. 3, "The System of the World," p. 501).
[5] Francis Bacon, *The Advancement of Learning and New Atlantis (London 1951), p. 11 (The First Book, 1.3)*

Another contemporary of Newton was Thomas Burnet, who is best known for his work "*Telluris Theoria Sacra, or Sacred Theory of the Earth.*"

Commenting on Burnet's book in January 1681, Newton offered "by way of conjecture" a view of how the planets might have been arranged by God in an initial act of creation and their motion steadily accelerated until the desired tempo for their coordinated movements had been reached[6].

Post Newtonian Cosmology

Modern cosmologists, or scientists who study the nature of the universe no longer necessarily agree with Newton as it relates to the way in which events take place. In other words, Newton saw the universe as infinite and changeless, while the modern scientist views it as evolving, expanding, being, and yet its origins are still a mystery to them.

In 1894, Albert Michelson (no relation to the author) delivered an address at the dedication of the Ryerson Physical Laboratory at the University of Chicago. In his address, he stated, *"The more important fundamental laws and facts of physical science have all been discovered."*

Imagine that even in 1894 the physics community did not think there was much new to learn about the universe.

---

[6] Newton, *Correspondence, ii (1960), 329-34*

Yet, it was only ten years later that another Albert, this time Einstein revolutionized and changed the way the world looked at the universe when he gave us E=mc². The beauty of this story is that Einstein's breakthrough was based on Michelson's previous work.

In 1929, Edwin Hubble, whom the famed NASA Hubble Space Telescope is named after, discovered the expansion of the universe by showing that the more distant a galaxy is from us the faster it is moving away. It was also the first observational support for a new theory on the origin of the universe proposed by Georges Lemaitre: **the Big Bang.** After all, an expanding Universe must once have been smaller. Lemaître was a pioneer in applying Albert Einstein's theory of general relativity to cosmology. In a 1927 article, which preceded Edwin Hubble's landmark article by two years, Lemaître derived what became known as Hubble's law.

Scientific Account of Creation

As previously mentioned, the branch of science that deals with the origin of the universe is known as cosmology. Throughout history and in every culture humankind would look up at the sky and wonder: What was the origin of the sun, the moon and the stars?

The concept of Creation ex nihilo, or in Hebrew *"yesh me'ayin[7]"* presents the perfect contrast. Ayin in Hebrew comes from *Ein* (not), which relates to nothingness. While it is contrasted with the term *"Yesh,"* which means "something/exist/being/is"). This concept is considered to be impossible, because science asserts that something cannot be created from nothing.

Therefore, secular scientists view the universe as eternal, and in this way they neatly avoid any questions regarding its origin. The biblical account that the universe was ***created*** became an arena of conflict between science and religion. This conflict remained intact for many years.

However, the conflict that existed has slowly changed over time, and evolved as we reached the twentieth century. The work of scientists like Michelson and Einstein coupled with Astronomers like Hubble brought about an unprecedented explosion of scientific knowledge that was nowhere more dramatic, than in study of the universe. Astronomers studying the heavenly bodies had been doing so in order to chart the paths of the stars, planets and comets. They were more concerned with determining their composition, spectrum and other properties, rather than determining their origin.

They seemed to be satisfied with the mystery of origin. Now, advances in cosmology during the past few decades have, for the first time, allowed many scientists to construct an understandable history of the origin of the universe. Today, an overwhelming body of scientific evidence supports the big bang theory of cosmology.

---

[7] Something from nothing

There are four pieces of evidence that the supporters of the big bang theory use as proof:

1. The discovery of the remnant of the initial ball of light that fills the universe;

2. The hydrogen-to-helium ratio in the universe;

3. The expansion of the galaxies;

4. The perfect black-body spectrum of the microwave background radiation measured by the COBE space satellite in 1990, and the additional measurements of this radiation made by the MAP space satellite launched in 2001.

You hear such quotes as *"The big bang theory works better than ever,"*[8] or, *"The modern theory of cosmic origins [asserts] that the universe erupted from an enormously energetic event...the big bang theory of creation is referred to as the standard model of cosmology."*[9] The most important assertion of the big bang theory is that *the universe was literally created.* It is instructive to quote some of the world's foremost authorities. Nobel laureate Paul Dirac, a major architect of twentieth-century physics, writes: *"It seems certain that there was a definite time of creation."*

---
[8] George Musser, "Four Keys to Cosmology," *Scientific American* (February 2004): 30.
[9] Greene, *The Elegant Universe* (London, 1999), 345-346.

Leading cosmologist Stephen Hawking writes: *"The creation lies outside the scope of the presently known laws of physics."*

When cosmologists use the term **"creation,"** to what are they referring? Precisely what object was created? Scientists have discovered that the universe began with the sudden appearance of an enormous ball of light, called the "primeval light-ball." This "explosion of light" was dubbed the "big bang" by the British astrophysicist Fred Hoyle. The remnant of this primeval light-ball was first detected in 1965 by two American physicists, Arno Penzias and Robert Wilson, who were awarded the Nobel Prize for physics for their discovery.

Does The Gap Narrow?

In more recent studies, we are finding scientists who have written at length about what they consider an emerging harmony between the spiritual account of creation and the discoveries of modern science.

Books have been written, such as those by Nathan Aviezer, *In the Beginning...Biblical Creation & Science* (New Jersey, 1990) and *Fossils and Faith* (New Jersey, 2002); Gerald Schroeder, *Genesis and the Big Bang: The Discovery of Harmony Between Modern Science and the Bible*(New York, 1990) and *The Science of G-d: The Convergence of Scientific and Biblical Wisdom* (New York, 1997); Yehudah Levi, *Facing Current Challenges* (New York, 1998) and *Science in Torah: The Scientific Knowledge of the Talmudic Sages* (New York, 2004).

In these books, our authors bring strong evidence from the "Big Bang" theory of cosmology, narrowing the gap between spirituality and science. Now that they have accepted the notion that the universe is not eternal, but had a beginning, they have begun to tackle such issues as, the age of the universe, the origins of life, and most importantly the issue of design. In other words, if the universe had a beginning, and if we can age the universe, and discuss the origins of life in general and humankind in particular, do we have to also deal with the possibility that the universe had an architect, a designer, or creator?

The dichotomy that exists in this argument is one of nature versus divinity. First, if we are going to consider what type of evidence can be uncovered through the lens of the natural world, we have to ask the following questions:

1. Does science have limits? Within the framework of this question, we can ask further if science has the ability of proving a theory with such proof, that it is no longer open to challenge or review?

This has always been the challenge for science, and as the gap narrows, more and more people question science's ability to answer all the questions of our present reality

2. What does the evidence that science brings forth actually tell us?

There is much evidence being presented by modern scientists in the areas of cosmology astronomy, genetics and science. Based on their current theories, do they either narrow the gap or widen the gap between the concepts of evolution and intelligent design?

These and other questions are what we hope to uncover as we delve deeper into the Science of Kabbalah!

Review Questions

1. What is the definition of the Hebrew word Kabbalah?

2. Is Kabbalah a Religion?

3. Who was one of the first scientists to connect secular science with the wisdom of Kabbalah?

4. On what did Sir Isaac Newton base most of his scientific research?

5. What was Newton's view of the universe?

6. How did modern cosmology differ in their view of the universe?

7. Who first discovered the expansion of the universe?

8. How has the acceptance of the "Big Bang Theory" narrowed the gap between modern science and spirituality?

Review Answers

1. Kabbalah means "receiving." This is a very important concept to pay attention to as we move forward through this course. The concept of "reception" is a foundational principle in the science of Kabbalah.

2. Kabbalah is not a religion; it is a science. As you look over the next lesson, you will see how the gap that exists between the secular and spiritual has narrowed in the world of science.

3. Sir Isaac Newton was not only a scientist, but a theologian. As such he chose to study many of the Jewish texts, and it is believed that many of his mathematical formulas were based on the science of Kabbalah

4. According to the records that are archived at Trinity College in Cambridge, it said that his scientific research is based on philosophical principles

5. Newton saw the universe as infinite and changeless. While this does not line up completely with the modern scientific view of an eternal universe, it is closer to the pre big bang theory view of science. One would not have expected such a view from a scientist who was also a theologian.

6. Modern cosmology viewed the universe as eternal. In a sense, they almost had to do so, in order to avoid the question of its origin. If it was eternal, they would not have to explain how it came into creation.

7. Edwin Hubble in 1929 discovered the expansion of the universe by showing that the more distant a galaxy is from us the faster it is moving away. It was the first time in history that any observational proof could be shown for the theory of Georges Lemaitre's, **Big Bang.** The Hubble telescope is also named after him.

8. Many modern scientists have written extensively on the "Big Bang" theory of cosmology. They have rejected the idea that universe is eternal. By accepting the theory that the universe had a beginning, they have begun to tackle such issues as, the age of the universe, the origins of life, and most importantly the issue of design. This has allowed for a narrowing of the gap between spirituality and science.

Science of Kabbalah – Lesson Two
The Significance of Light

Written by: Rabbi Yitzchak Michaelson

164 Village Path, Lakewood NJ 08701 732.370.3344
164 Rabbi Akiva, Bnei Brak, 03.616.6340

Outline of This Lesson:

1. Why Care about a SuperNova

2. The Significance of Light

3. The Interaction of Light and Time

4. Quantum Mechanics

5. Review Answers

6. Review Questions

Why Care about Supernovae

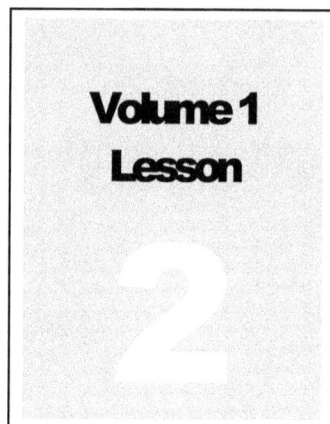

Volume 1 Lesson 2

Previously we noted that Frank E. Manuel in his book *"The Religion of Isaac Newton,"* quoted that Galileo and Kepler had based their fundamental arguments on an ancient dictum of scriptural interpretation by the Jewish sages: ***"The Bible speaks in the language of everyman."***

Kepler was a mathematician, astrologer, and astronomer. He is best known for his "Laws of Planetary Motion," which Isaac Newton used to develop his theory of universal gravitation. Another well known event that took place in Kepler's life was SN 1604 or Kepler's Super Nova. A supposed new star, that appeared in the night skies.

It would take just over 380 years for another such event to take place. It took place at approximately 3 a.m. the morning of February 24, 1987, when from an observatory in the Chilean mountains the first Supernova since SN 1604 appeared in the night skies. Astronomers could not believe what they were seeing at first. When they realized what it was, they also came to realize it was the closest observed supernova since 1604.

Those fortunate enough to be in the Earth's Southern Hemisphere could actually witness this event. This supernova remained visible to the eye for many months and has been studied in the decades since.

Supernova 1987A was the brightest supernova seen from Earth in the four centuries since the telescope was invented. The explosion occurred 160,000 years ago, on the outskirts of the Tarantula Nebula in the Large Magellanic Cloud – a nearby dwarf galaxy.

The light of the explosion – traveling at 186,000 miles per second (300 million meters per second) – finally reached Earth on February 24, 1987.

It could still be seen for many months, until around May of 1987 when it started to decline in brightness. However, this was the first time that astronomers were given sort of a bird's-eye view of a supernova. As a result, science has uncovered many incredible insights into these phenomena.

The word *nova* means *new star*. Early astronomers like Kepler thought he was witnessing the birth of a star when he first saw the supernova that now bears his name – Kepler's Star – in 1604. As we said, Kepler's star was the last close and observable one, but it was before the invention of the telescope. What is the difference? With the invention of the telescope we have learned that what is being witnessed is not the birth of a start, but instead the death of one.

What have we learned from the death of Supernova 1987a? According to NASA[1] Supernova's like 1987a can stir up surrounding gas and trigger formation of new stars and planets.

---

[1] National Aeronautics and Space Administration

The gas from which these stars and planets form will be enriched with elements such as carbon, nitrogen, oxygen, and iron, which are the components for all known life. That statement alone if simply amazing.

What does this have to do with Stardust? One would think we are speaking about movies, book titles, or children's fairy tales. However, stardust is no joking matter, and in the grand scheme of science plays a much bigger role in how we view the universe and our own existence.

Why care about supernovae? There are some good reasons!

1. We are made of stardust. When you hear this common phrase amongst modern physicists, you must think it is a joke, as I said. However, both astronomers and physicists today believe that a large fraction of the atoms in our bodies were forged inside stars. That the stardust produced by Supernovae like 1987a when dispersed into space are the mechanism by which the atoms created in stars are the same atoms which make up our physical bodies today.

2. High-energy radiation and how life evolves. Astronomers also believe that Supernovae in the Milky Way galaxy produce the type of high energy radiation that could have contributed to the background radiation that produces mutation and evolution of species on Earth.

3. A cosmic trigger to our local solar system. There is intriguing evidence that a supernova triggered the formation of our own solar system – our sun, Earth and the other planets near us in space – five billion years ago. For all these reasons and more, astronomers want to know what makes supernovae explode and what happens after they do.

You may be saying to yourself right now that this all sounds quite amazing, but how does it tie in with Kabbalah, and what we call the narrowing gap between science and spirituality?

I promise you, that we are currently laying the foundation to answer that very question. In order to understand such ancient wisdom one must first be willing to examine all the evidence produced for what we call creation.

The Significance of Light

In the previous section we discussed Supernova 1987a and how the explosion occurred 160,000 years ago, on the outskirts of the Tarantula Nebula in the Large Magellanic Cloud – a nearby dwarf galaxy. The light of the explosion – traveling at 186,000 miles per second (300 million meters per second) – finally reached Earth at 3 a.m. February 24, 1987.

That basically tells us that this supernova was approximately 160.000 light years from our Earth. This means that the explosion took place 160,000 years ago and it was only after 160,000 years that those photons reached us and made SN1987a visible, in the early morning hours of February 24th. How in the world does one make sense of this?

The only way to make sense of such a concept is to understand the science of light, and how it relates to the speed of light. Not only that, but how light affects time.

Until the last two centuries it was virtually impossible to understand the dynamics and science of light. Then, within a short period of time several discoveries were made that allowed us to better understand the nature of light and its physical properties. Of course, we know that the light we experience comes from the Sun and from stars as well, in our universe.

We initially learned about electricity and magnetism through the work of a Scottish physicist named James Maxwell. Maxwell determined that electricity produces magnetism and then that magnetism produces electricity. He was the first to coin the phrase *"electromagnetic,"* where previously these two forces were considered completely separate from one another. As a result of his research, science uncovered the dualistic nature of light. The simple explanation is that light is made up of both electric and magnetic energy.

There are photons of light that travel to us from the Sun and stars, as both particles and waves.

Another scientist appeared on the scene and discovered that there were additional forms of electromagnetic energy in addition to light. His name was Heinrich Rudolph Hertz and what he discovered were radio waves. This research led to the discovery of other's like x-rays, gamma rays, micro waves, and ultra violent, to name a few. All of these forms of electromagnetic energy are measured by frequency and wavelength.

These were amazing discoveries and led to many important explanations for the science of light. However, this also produced a paradox for many scientists. As I mentioned before, light has not only wave like properties, but can also be particles. In one sense this contradicts the wave-like properties of light. Since we are not really interested in going into complicated explanations on how this is possible, suffice it to say that better minds, meaning top scientists are still mystified by this concept. This does not surprise me, as our goal is to continue to understand the narrowing gap between science and spirituality.

Einstein actually tried to make sense of this duality that seemed to defy logic, by stating that the particles were photons and a flow of photons were a wave. That is how he made sense of the contradiction.

Brian Greene, the author of the now classic book The Elegant Universe states, "The microscopic world demands that we shed our intuition that something is either a wave or a particle and embrace the possibility that it is both... We can utter words such as "wave-particle duality."

We can translate these words into mathematical formulization that describes the real-world experiments with amazing accuracy. But it is extremely hard to understand at a deep intuitive level this dazzling feature of the microscopic world"[2]

The truth is, while Einstein had his theory and as brilliant as all of the scientists in the world are, no one really understands it or can explain it. Science has had no problem efficiently harnessing electromagnetic energy.

They have been at the fore front of creating much of the technology that we simple folk take for granted every day. At the same time, the world of science almost daily has to come to terms with how mysterious and paradoxical the physical world is. This of course is no surprise to people of faith, and those who accept that science is simply unwilling to recognize that the gap is narrowing.

---

[2] page 103; Vintage Books, 1999; New York

In the world of spirituality we have concepts of both hidden light, and revealed light. It is interesting to note, that a similar concept exists within science when discussing light. When you take into consideration the dualistic nature of particle and wave form, the way in which it mimics the hidden and revealed in spirituality is based on its measurement. Meaning that light only reveals itself according to one of these two features at a time, but not both simultaneously. So, it is astonishing to learn that if measured in wave form that is how light will be revealed, and yet if measured as particles it will only reveal itself in that way.

After the discoveries made about light, the world of physics realized that another one of the building blocks of all matter exhibited this same type of paradoxical duality. Simply stated "atoms" display this same wave-particle duality. Consider that from the largest supernova to the smallest particle, everything made of matter is made of atoms that exhibit the same phenomenon we described about light. However, the discoveries did not end there.

The Interaction of Light and Time

Previously, we discussed the 1987a Supernova and specifically how it was approximately 160,000 light years away from us. As we described, it literally took 160,000 years for the light of the death of that star to reach earth at precisely the time it was both photographed by telescope and seen by the naked eye in the Southern Hemisphere.

Now, that we understand a little bit about the science of light, we need to learn more about how light and time interact in order to make sense of this 160,000 year period.

What we know from science is that light travels at the speed of 186,000 miles per second. In order to make sense of the amount of time it will take an object to reach a destination we have to know whether the destination is moving or stationary.

Let's use a football analogy to try to understand the above point. When a quarterback is throwing the ball to a receiver, the amount of time it takes for the ball to reach the receiver is based on whether he is running towards or away from the quarterback.

So for instance, if the receiver runs a pattern and realizes that he is in coverage, then he might run back towards the quarterback to be open to receive a pass. Obviously, if he is running toward the quarterback the ball will reach him much faster than if he was running toward the goal line.

However, light is not a football and is not subject to this same example. So, let's get back to our Supernova and consider for a moment the journey that the light took to arrive exactly at a certain spot on the earth to be visible at 3 a.m. the morning of February 24th, 1987.

Could we posit that if a Neanderthal was peering up at the sky some 160,000 years ago, he would have seen the light? What about even 5,000 years ago in the Bronze Age, could someone have viewed the light?

If you were even to believe for instance that there was other intelligent life living closer to the supernova that wanted to race towards us to warn us, you would have to realize the impossibility of such a notion. Why? Because nothing can travel faster than the speed of light!

So, I have a question for you to take a few minutes to ponder on. **If you, yes you, were somehow able to have been in some type of futuristic space ship that left at the same time as the light from Supernova 1987a and were able to travel alongside of it for that 160,000 year journey, how much time would have passed when you arrived at the same spot at 3 a.m. on the morning of February 24th, 1987?**

Are you ready for the answer?

Exactly zero time would have passed! That's right, as incomprehensible as that sounds, not years, months, days, hours, or even seconds would have passed. The best explanation I have heard on this subject is from Dr. Gerald Schroeder in his book "The Science of God." Dr. Schroeder states as follows:

"The difference in the perception of the flow of time at the speed of light is not a quantitative difference from a lot of time (160,000 years) to a much shorter time, however short that period might be. The difference in the flow of time is a qualitative difference, the difference between our existence where all events occur through an unceasing temporally linear flow and an existence in which time does not exist. From that perspective, all the developments that took place during the 160,000 years occurred simultaneously.

Past, present and future had blended into an eternal, ever-present, unending NOW. Light you see is outside of time, a fact of nature proven in thousands of experiments at hundreds of universities."[3]

The conclusion that one draws from the above statement is that light, at least as it relates to the speed of light, actually exists outside of the realm of time. Schroeder would refer to this as an "eternal now." Think about how far we have come in our study thus far. Remember, in earlier times the scientists in the days of Newton even though they were also theologians, could not wrap their minds around the universe being eternal. The stumbling block in many cases has really not been science, but religion. Anyone who is willing to do the research will soon find that it is in fact science and scientists that are proving spirituality, rather than the religionists.

If we look back at Einstein's laws of relativity they not only proved that space, time, and matter are not constant, but changing. In addition, we explained also about the difference between particles and waves, and how they are viewed in the way that one chooses to observe them.

Why is it important to know such things? Because when you understand this science, you realize that Einstein came up with both theories and laws that have proven to be correct. One of the most significant as it relates to our study is the fact that the faster one travels relative to another object, like in our make believe ship traveling alongside the light from Supernova 1987a, the slower time flows. So much so, that at the speed of light, which is the highest speed attainable, time ceases.

---

[3] The Science of God – the Convergence of Scientific and Biblical Wisdom, Gerald L. Schroeder, Broadway Books, page 164

Thus, Einstein's laws of relativity have proven not through some theological formula based on the bible that a timeless existence is proven out, but instead it is through science.

Now, this does not mean we want the reader to come away with the idea that there is not a spiritual component to what we have shared so far. On the contrary, we are merely providing the scientific proof that supports spirituality. We will explore in much more detail in upcoming lessons how the concept of light effects what we know of as creation, as well as other concepts.

Keep in mind moving forward that we do not pretend to understand how yesterday, last week, last month, and next year all can exist in what we described as this "eternal now," but in the context of the speed of light they do, as we have proven through science that no time passes.

Finally, before we spend a little time on quantum mechanics, I think it is significant to state that when considering the big bang theory and Supernovae, that one has to admit that light was in fact the first creation of the universe.

Based on the above statement, we can further posit that although we live in a world that is made up of time, space, and matter, there is a spiritual link to the eternity that is our universe. Simply stated, light exists outside of time and space.

Bringing it full circle back to $E=MC^2$, we have learned that all the different forms of light, whether photons, gamma rays, x-rays, microwaves, or microwaves are able to actually disregard their timelessness as an energy source by transforming into matter. This allows it to enter into the realm of time and space.

Schroeder goes on to explain this in the comparison of light being both energy and matter in the same way that both steam and ice are also water, each being two forms of the same thing.

You will find yourself coming back to this lesson, as we will discuss light and its interaction with creation in future lessons. Now on to a little bit on the concept of quantum mechanics, which is also related to both Newtonian and Einstein' cosmology.

Quantum Mechanics

In Lesson 1 we discussed the impact that Albert Einstein had on post Newton cosmology, and we cannot emphasize enough how his theory of relativity chan the way we understand the universe.

While many may not necessarily understand the formula, who has not hear Einstein's famous equation $E=MC^2$ mentioned many times already. The for breaks down as follows, (E [energy] = M [mass] x C [velocity of light] squ This revealed to us that energy and matter are two sides of the same coin ar exchangeable. It is through the knowledge $E=MC^2$, of converting relatively amounts of matter into enormous amounts of energy, that atomic po' produced.

What is revolutionary for the purposes of our science of Kabbalah, is he formula reveals ideas that we will present in much further detail moving for

As to not jump too far ahead, consider that each one of us is a vessel, and as vessels we are in essence matter, and as matter we are also considered a condensed form or light, which is energy.

We have not even touched on the fact that quantum mechanics also has an effect on other sciences. So much so, that there are completely new fields of study like quantum biology. For instance, consider that every year there are thousands of European Robins that head south for the winter. They travel some 2000 miles, however, it is the way in which they navigate that is a spectacular wonder. Why? Well, these Robins do not navigate this journey like other migratory species that use landmarks, ocean currents, or the sun. These birds are actually able to detect the Earth's magnetic field.

However, that is not all. Not only can they detect this magnetic field, which by the way is about 100 times weaker that that fridge magnet you brought back from your last vacation, but it seems they are actually able to see the magnetic field as well. The process by which they accomplish this was described by Albert Einstein as "spooky." It seems that these Robins have a built-in compass that uses this spooky form of quantum mechanics.

If you compare the laws of quantum mechanics, this new field of quantum biology along with the other formulas and explanations thus far presented, you can begin to understand how we can claim that the gap has narrowed between science and spirituality.

In fact, in the same way that we describe matter and energy being two sides of the same coin, and that these types of duality are paradoxical, we can also say that the realms of the spiritual and the physical are not unrelated, but are intrinsically united. Based on this, we can also say that nothing represents truth more than the concept of light.

Having become famous for his brilliance, and arguably one of the greatest physicists in history, Einstein spent the next 30 years of his life on a quest to produce a unified field theory. This unified field theory would in essence combine gravity and electromagnetism into a single theory.

His motivation seemed to be driven by the need to prove that the forces of nature were somehow unified. In his Nobel Prize lecture of 1923 he stated, *"The intellect seeking after an integrated theory cannot rest content with the assumption there exist two distinct fields totally independent of each other by their nature."*

Besides his drive to prove unified field theory, he believed there was a need to answer the paradoxes that existed within quantum mechanics[4] in order to unify them into a theory that included gravity and electromagnetism.

Einstein ultimately failed in his quest for a unified field theory, but it did not stop him from working even until his dying day.

---

[4] Quantum mechanics (QM; also known as quantum physics, quantum theory, the wave mechanical model, or matrix mechanics), including quantum field theory, is a fundamental theory in physics which describes nature at the smallest scales of energy levels of atoms and subatomic particles. Feynman, Richard; Leighton, Robert; Sands, Matthew (1964). The Feynman Lectures on Physics, Vol. 3. California Institute of Technology. p. 1.1.

Many believe his failure came from his rejection of quantum mechanics, which distanced him from the other physicists of his day. Based on the following quote in 1954, the year before he died, it would appear he was very much aware of his position. *"I must seem like an ostrich who forever buries its head in the relativistic sand in order not to face the evil quanta."*[5]

Others believe his failure came as a result of him being ahead of his time. That the tools needed to prove such a theory were not available before his death. The greatest paradox to me is that while physicists have made great strides in the field of science, none have yet been able to come up with a testable and provable theory, even following in Einstein's footsteps.

I say paradox, because it is my belief that the answers, and science they have been searching for has been available for thousands of years. They are simply looking in the wrong place. Like Newton and his peers, and even those who came after who were willing to look at this ancient wisdom, one must look to the science of Kabbalah for such answers. A science based on ignoring this physical reality in order to unlock the world of spirituality.

It is only in the spiritual realm that one can bring true unification, where all paradoxes fade away.

---

[5] Plural of quantum

Review Questions

1. What is a Supernova?

2. What is one of the main pieces of information that was learned from SN 1987a related to our known universe?

3. How can scientists believe in the fairytale, that we are made of stardust?

4. We know from out study that not only in science, but in the spiritual world, there is the concept of both revealed light and hidden light. How do we reconcile the two?

5. If SN 1987a was 160,000 light years away, how much time would pass if you were able to travel at the same speed and arrive at the same time at 3 a.m. on February 24th?

6. What does Einstein's formula $E=MC^2$ teach us about time as it relates to lights ability to exist as both energy and matter?

7. What other forms of science have been established based on the science of quantum mechanics?

Review Answers

1. Kepler, one of the early mathematicians and astronomers was the one who first found SN 1604, also known as Kepler's Super Nova, a new star that appeared in the night sky. However, it was not actually a new star as many had assumed for so many years. Instead after future research related to SN1987a, it was learned that in fact, this was the death of a star.

2. According to NASA Supernova's like 1987a can stir up surrounding gas and trigger formation of new stars and planets. The gas from which these stars and planets form will be enriched with elements such as carbon, nitrogen, oxygen, and iron, which are the components for all known life. In other words, the death of a star like this gives us some insight to the truth about how the big bang theory closes the gap between science and spirituality. As we can see from the components that sustain life being formed as a result of such an explosion.

3. While it sounds like something from a poem, or Joni Mitchell song, science has proved otherwise. Both astronomers and physicists today believe that a large fraction of the atoms in our bodies were forged inside stars. That the stardust produced by Supernovae, like 1987a when dispersed into space are the mechanism by which the atoms created in stars are the same atoms which make up our physical bodies today.

After all, when you ponder the answer to question 2, realizing that all the components that are able to sustain life come from events such as this, it is not too far a stretch to believe that we are in fact made of stardust.

4. It is very easy to reconcile the dual nature of light in science and spirituality. In our study, we learned that just as there is hidden and revealed light in the world of spirituality, in science light has a dual nature. Light exist in both particle and wave form, and in this way it mimics the hidden and revealed. Meaning that light only reveals itself according to one of the two features at a time, but not both simultaneously. So, it is astonishing to learn that if measured in wave form that is how it will be revealed, and yet if measured as particles it will only reveal itself in that way.

5. In our lesson we discussed the fact that light, at least as it relates to the speed of light, actually exists outside of the realm of time. Dr. Gerald Schroeder would refer to this as an "eternal now." In other words, when you are discussing the concept of the speed of light there is no past, present, or future. There is only Now!

6. We have learned that all the different forms of light, whether photons, gamma rays, x-rays, microwaves, or microwaves are able to actually disregard their timelessness as an energy source, by transforming into matter. This allows it to enter into the realm of time and space. Dr. Schroeder goes on to explain this in the comparison of light being both energy and matter in the same way that both steam and ice are also water, each being two forms of the same thing.

7. One new field of study is actually quantum biology. We used the example of thousands of European Robins that head south for the winter. They travel some 2000 miles navigating not as other similar species by using ocean currents or the sun and stars. Instead they not only actually able to detect the Earth's magnetic field, but have a particular protein in their eye that allows them to also see the Earth's magnetic field. This is spooky science according to Einstein, because these birds actually in a way experience the duality of both particles and waves.

www.ingramcontent.com/pod-product-compliance
Lightning Source LLC
Chambersburg PA
CBHW062055090426
42740CB00016B/3146